YOUR TEETH

Joan Iveson-Iveson

Illustrated by Bill Donohoe

All About You

Your Eyes
Your Hands and Feet
Your Health
Your Nose and Ears
Your Skin and Hair
Your Teeth

Acknowledgements

All the photographs in this book were supplied by Sally and Richard Greenhill, with the exception of the following: Jim Merrett 16, 20.

First published in 1985 by Wayland (Publishers) Limited
49 Lansdowne Place, Hove, East Sussex BN3 1HF, England
© 1985 Wayland (Publishers) Limited

ISBN 0 85078 515 4

Phototypeset by Kalligraphics Limited, Redhill, Surrey
Printed in Italy by G. Canale and C.S.p.A., Turin
Bound in the UK by Hunter & Foulis Ltd, Edinburgh

Contents

What are teeth for?

Your teeth are very important. Without them you couldn't eat all the things you enjoy, like a nice juicy hamburger, or a crunchy apple. With just **gums** you would be like a baby, living on liquids and mashed-up foods.

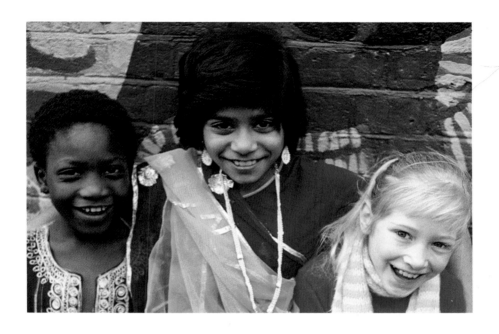

Not everybody's teeth look the same. Some people have big teeth, others have small or crooked teeth, or teeth with gaps. Teeth are not always white, sometimes they are nearly yellow.

Sharks grow new teeth all the time, but you cannot do that. Your teeth must last a lifetime. To look after them properly you should first find out all about them.

Baby teeth

Everyone has two sets of teeth in their lifetime. The first set are called 'milk' or 'baby' teeth. Their proper name is deciduous teeth. A deciduous tree loses its leaves in autumn, and these first teeth will also be lost later on.

A baby's teeth

1 incisor
2 incisor
3 canine
4 molar

There are 20 of them and they have different names. They begin to appear when you are about 6 months old. Until then they are hidden away inside the jaw bones. They push through the gums, two at a time. This is called **teething**. By the time a baby is 18 months old he may have nearly all his first teeth.

Teething can be painful and a baby is given hard things to bite and chew on to help the teeth come through.

Adult teeth

You do not keep your baby teeth. They first begin to grow loose and fall out when you are about 6. Hidden away in the gums are the adult, or permanent teeth. Because you are growing all the time there is more room in your mouth, and you will have 32 adult teeth. The last of them will come through when you are about 21.

An adult's teeth

1 incisor
2 incisor
3 canine
4 premolar
5 premolar
6 molar
7 molar
8 wisdom tooth

The first baby teeth to come out are the front teeth. Teeth have always been thought of as a bit magical. Many children put their lost tooth under their pillow at night, hoping the tooth fairy will take it and leave some money behind.

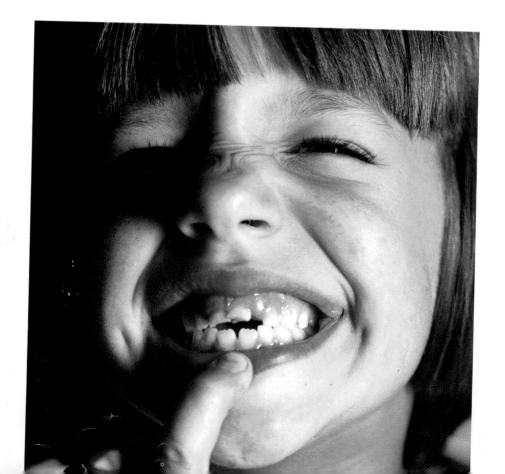

What are teeth made of?

Your teeth fit into sockets, or holes, in your jaw bones. The sockets are covered on the outside by your gums. The teeth can move very slightly inside the sockets. This means they will not be damaged if you bite on something like a very hard sweet.

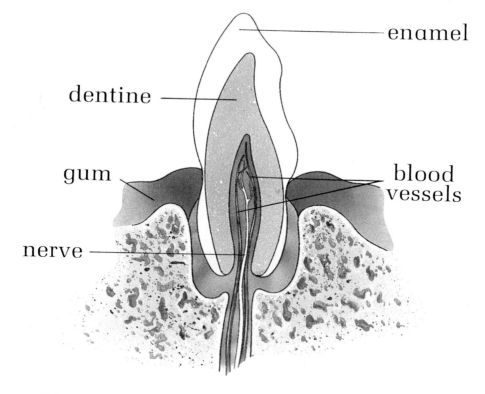

enamel

dentine

gum

blood vessels

nerve

This drawing looks right inside a tooth. The outside is made of **enamel,** the hardest material in your body. Underneath is dentine, which is like bone. In the centre is the soft part where the **nerves** and **blood vessels** are. The blood keeps the tooth alive, and the nerves send messages to the brain and also get information from it. Your nerves tell your brain when you have toothache.

The work they do

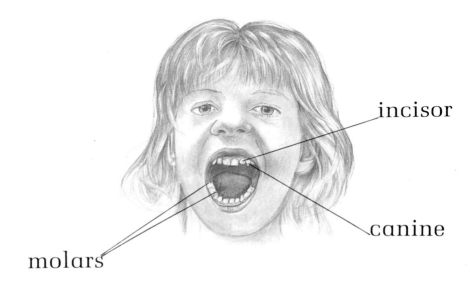

incisor

canine

molars

Your teeth are not all the same shape and size. Different teeth have different jobs to do when they chew up your food. If you look at the drawing you can see the different teeth. The **incisors**, or front teeth, and **canines** are sharp, and cut and tear your food. The **molars** are flatter and bumpy, and they grind up your food ready to swallow.

When you are eating, your teeth all work together to mash your food up into smaller and smaller pieces, and mix it with spit. Saliva is the proper name for the watery liquid you can feel in your mouth. It helps soften the food so you can swallow it easily. Saliva helps keep your mouth clean and also helps you to talk. Sometimes you cannot speak when you are frightened because the saliva in your mouth dries up.

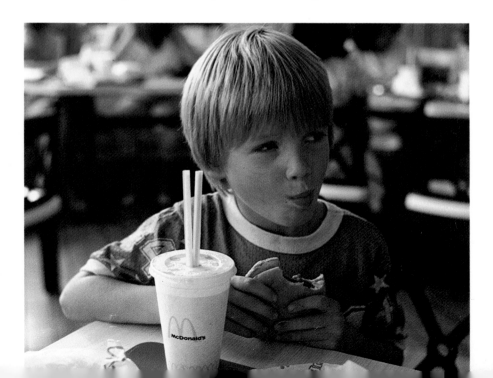

Why teeth go bad

Animals nearly always keep their teeth all their lives. People are not so lucky. Can you think why? It has to do with what you eat and drink. Unlike animals, most people like to eat lots of sweet, sugary foods. Sugar is bad for your teeth and causes holes to form. This is called tooth decay.

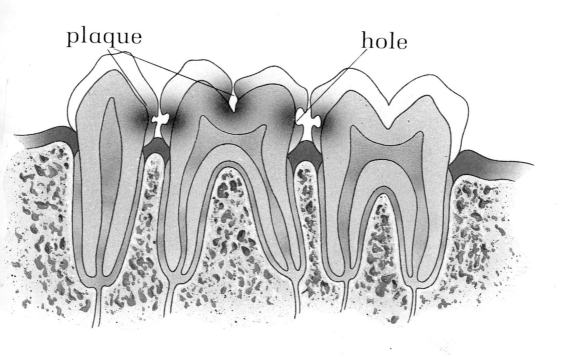

plaque   hole

This drawing shows where tooth decay has happened. Tiny germs, called bacteria, live in your mouth and feed on the sugar you eat. This makes a sticky stuff called **plaque** which clings to your teeth. Plaque attacks the hard outside of your teeth and begins to make tiny holes in it. The holes will not mend by themselves. After a while they will get bigger and bigger. Only the dentist can stop the damage.

Cleaning your teeth

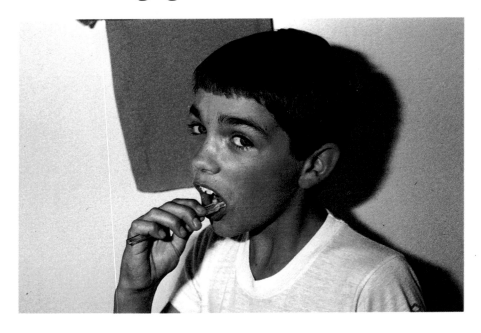

Do you always clean your teeth properly? You should brush them twice a day — after breakfast and at bedtime. You need your own toothbrush with a small head and nylon medium-hard bristles. If you can, you should buy a new one every month. You must never let anyone else use it.

Choose toothpaste which has **fluoride** in it. Fluoride strengthens the hard enamel on the outside of your teeth. You can also buy fluoride mouthwash. Last, you can use disclosing tablets. These stain your teeth red in the places where there is plaque, the sticky stuff that makes holes in your teeth.

When you are ready to brush your teeth, make sure you have a good light to see by and a big mirror in front of you. Get your mouthwash and discloser ready and then squeeze some toothpaste onto your brush. Begin with your teeth together. Hold the brush so all the bristles are against your teeth. Start brushing round the outside of your teeth.

fluoride
mouthwash

disclosing
tablets

fluoride
toothpaste

Move your toothbrush round and round in
small circles. Then open your mouth and
brush the insides of your teeth. Brush the
biting and chewing surfaces too. Doing this
properly takes five minutes. Now use the
mouthwash and rinse carefully. Lastly use a
disclosing tablet. If there are any red stains
left after rinsing your mouth, you must brush
your teeth again!

Visiting the dentist

Your dentist looks after your teeth, and checks them carefully with special instruments. An **x-ray** might be taken to look right inside your jaw. A dentist will tell you the best way to clean your teeth, and what foods are good and bad for them. If your teeth are not growing straight

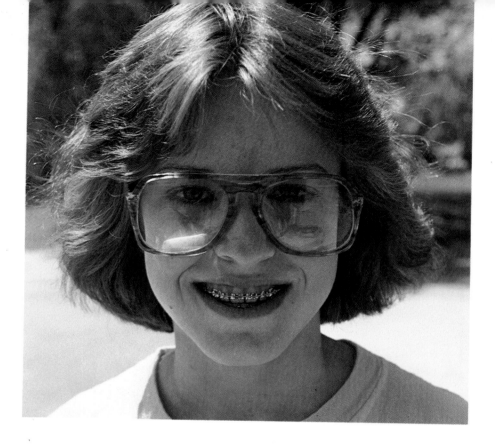

you may need a special wire **brace** fitted for
a while. Sometimes you will need a **filling** to
mend a hole in your tooth. First the dentist
may give you an injection to 'freeze' your
mouth so you won't feel anything. The tooth
is then drilled to make room for the metal
filling. After that the filling is put in.

Looking after your teeth

Now you know how important your teeth are. They need looking after if you are going to keep them until you are old. There is a lot to remember about what is good and what is bad for them. The list opposite will help you.

Caring about your teeth means:

Cutting down on sugar and eating fruit sometimes instead of sweets.

Eating crunchy foods like apples, nuts, raw carrots.

Cleaning your teeth properly at least twice a day and especially before going to bed, using a fluoride toothpaste.

Using disclosing tablets and a fluoride mouthwash.

Going to the dentist every six months.

Not caring about your teeth means:

Eating too many foods with sugar in them like sweets, chocolate, cakes, jam, biscuits, ice-cream.

Using a worn-out old toothbrush.

Cleaning your teeth in ten seconds flat.

Not going to the dentist.

Word list

Blood vessels The tubes that carry blood around your body.

Brace This is made of wire and is fitted onto teeth to help straighten them.

Canines The four sharp teeth next to the incisors.

Enamel The hard, white covering of a tooth.

Fluoride Something that strengthens the enamel on teeth.

Filling This is put in by the dentist to mend a hole in a tooth.

Gums The firm, pink part around your teeth.

Incisors The four sharp front teeth.

Molars The flat, bumpy back teeth.

Nerves The 'wires' that carry messages to and from your brain.

Plaque A sticky film that clings to teeth.

Teething When the baby teeth begin to push through the gums.

X-ray A photograph taken by powerful rays that can pass through most things except metal and bone.

Index